DISCOVER
Fossils

by Barbara Brannon

Table of Contents

Introduction	2
Chapter 1 What Are Fossils?	4
Chapter 2 Where Are Fossils?	8
Chapter 3 How Do We Learn About Fossils?	14
Conclusion	18
Concept Map	20
Glossary	22
Index	24

Introduction

Fossils are from long ago.

▲ Fossils were animals. Fossils were plants.

Words to Know

animals

forests

fossils

insects

organisms

plants

See the Glossary on page 22.

Chapter 1

What Are Fossils?

Some fossils were **plants**.

▲ This fossil was a plant.

Some fossils were **animals**.

▲ This fossil was an animal.

Some fossils were **insects**.

▲ This fossil was an insect.

Chapter 1

Fossils were **organisms**.

▲ These fossils were organisms.

What Are Fossils?

Sometimes a fossil is an animal bone.
Sometimes a fossil is animal teeth.

bone

teeth

Chapter 2

Where Are Fossils?

Some fossils are in cliffs.

It's A Fact

People find fossils in cliffs and mountains. The fossils are from other places.

▲ This fossil is from an ocean.

▲ This fossil is in a cliff.

Some fossils are in mountains.

▲ This fossil is in a mountain.

Chapter 2

Some fossils are from **forests**.

▲ This leaf lived in a forest.

Where Are Fossils?

Some fossils are from rain forests.

▲ This plant lived in a rain forest.

11

Chapter 2

Some fossils are from lakes.

▲ This fish lived in a lake.

Some fossils are from rivers.

▲ This turtle lived in a river.

Some fossils are from oceans.

▲ This plant lived in an ocean.

Chapter 3

How Do We Learn About Fossils?

People pick up rocks. People see fossils.

▲ Fossils are in rocks.

People dig up rocks. People see fossils.

▲ Fossils are in rocks.

It's A Fact

The Dodo was a bird. No Dodos live today. We learn about the Dodo from fossils.

▲ Dodo bird

Chapter 3

People study rocks. People see fossils.

▲ Fossils are in rocks.

How Do We Learn About Fossils?

Conclusion

Fossils are in many places.

Concept Map

Fossils

What Are Fossils?

- plants
- animals
- insects
- organisms

Where Are Fossils?

- cliffs
- mountains
- forests
- rain forests
- lakes
- rivers
- oceans

How Do We Learn About Fossils?

pick up rocks
dig up rocks
study rocks

Glossary

animals living things that can move around

Some fossils were **animals**.

forests areas of trees, plants, and animals

Some fossils are from **forests**.

fossils parts of organisms from the past

Some **fossils** are in mountains.

insects animals with six legs

Some fossils were **insects**.

organisms living plants or animals

*Some fossils were **organisms**.*

plants living things that cannot move around

*Some fossils were **plants**.*

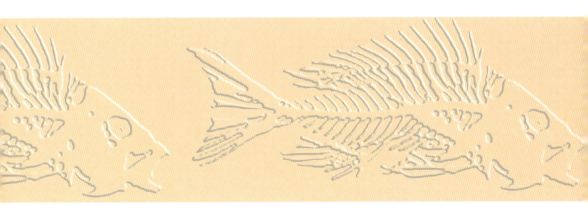

Index

animals, 2, 5, 7, 20

cliffs, 8, 20

forests, 10, 20

fossils, 2, 4–16, 18, 20–21

insects, 5, 20

lakes, 12, 20

mountains, 8, 9, 20

oceans, 8, 13, 20

organisms, 6, 20

plants, 2, 4, 11, 13, 20

rain forests, 11, 20

rivers, 13, 20

rocks, 14–16, 21

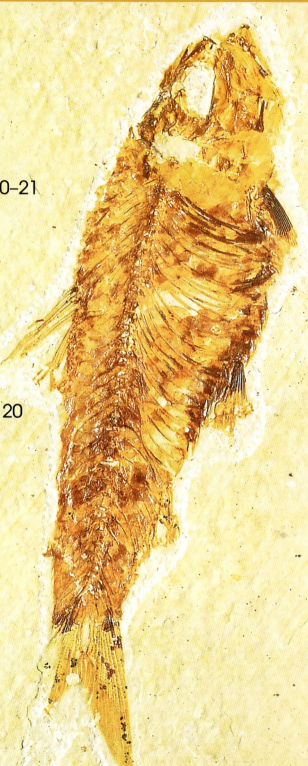